Words have wings,

So speak only good things

-Proverb

Copyright © 2025 Kathleen Rittson-Thomas. All rights reserved.
Cover and illustrations by Zoe Saunders.

No part of this publication may be reproduced in whole or in part, or stored in a retrieval system, or transmitted by any means, electronic, mechanical, photocopying, recording or otherwise, without written permission of the author.

Paperback ISBN: 978-0-473-75343-6
Hardcover ISBN: 978-0-473-75344-3

Meme loves to ride Big Red around her farm.

One day, she rode Big Red all the way to the end of her farm, to a corner she'd never been to before.

It was very pretty, and there was lovely, lush grassy pasture for the sheep and cattle to eat.

But she didn't know there was a swamp hidden in the grass, and she drove Big Red straight into it.

Big Red sank into the water, all the way up to the top of the wheels.

Meme had to climb off Big Red.

She tried to jump to solid ground, but she slipped and with a great big
SPLOSH
Meme fell right into the water.

Meme had to walk a long way back to the farmyard. Water sloshed in her boots, and her wet clothes stuck to her.

It was very uncomfortable!

Finally, she arrived at the farmyard.

She took Little Red out of the shed and drove along the lane, through the grassy pastures, until at last she reached the swamp where Big Red was stuck.

Meme tied a rope around Little Red's tow bar and then tied the other end of the rope to Big Red just between the two front wheels.

She hopped on Little Red and started the motor. The engine revved and revved, and Little Red pulled and pulled until, eventually, Big Red, all covered in mud, slowly came out of the swamp.

Hurray for Little Red!

At the farmyard, Meme washed Big Red and Little Red with warm soapy water until they were sparkling clean.

All is well on Meme's farm.

About the Author

Kathie Rittson-Thomas began farming later in life and writes stories for her grandchildren inspired by her real-life adventures on the farm.

She wrote this story to remind children that while challenges may feel overwhelming, there's a special kind of pride in solving problems on your own.

Thank you Zoe Saunders for your beautiful illustrations.

www.ingramcontent.com/pod-product-compliance
Lightning Source LLC
LaVergne TN
LVHW070613080526
838200LV00103B/350